FASCI
FACTS

TAYLOR SWIFT

Essential Trivia, Quotes, and Questions for Super-fans

Lyrica Taytor

WELCOME TO EVERYTHING TAYLOR SWIFT

Hey there, Swiftie! Are you ready to dive into the amazing world of Taylor Swift? This book is packed with 101 awesome facts about your favorite pop star, Taylor Swift! From her music and tours to her love of burritos and her incredible real estate adventures, we've got everything you need to become a Taylor Swift expert.

Did you know that Taylor Swift didn't try a burrito until she was 26 years old? Or that she made history at the American Music Awards as the female artist with the most wins ever? And there's more! Taylor's Eras Tour is like a musical journey through time, with over three hours of her biggest hits!

But wait, there's even more fun! Test your knowledge with trivia questions scattered throughout the book. Can you guess how many properties Taylor owns or the record she broke at the American Music Awards?

Get ready to explore the life of Taylor Swift, from her early days singing "The Star-Spangled Banner" at a basketball game to her dazzling fashion on the Eras Tour. Each fact is a peek into Taylor's world, showing us why she's not just a music icon but a real superstar in every way.

So, grab your spot and let's start this exciting journey through "101 Facts About Taylor Swift!" It's going to be a fun, fascinating, and totally Swift-tastic adventure!

Before you start

To make really test yourself I want you to write down any facts you already know about Taylor. It could be anything, and keep a look out through this book to see if we included it.

_____
_____
_____
_____
_____
_____
_____
_____
_____
_____
_____
_____
_____
_____
_____
_____
_____
_____
_____
_____
_____
_____
_____
_____
_____
_____
_____
_____
_____

01 Facts About Taylor

1. A Star is Born in 2006: Taylor Swift's First Single "Tim McGraw"

Taylor Swift released her debut single, "Tim McGraw," which marked the beginning of her remarkable journey in the world of music. The song not only introduced Taylor's unique style but also showcased her deep connection with country music. It was the first step in a career that would make her one of the most celebrated artists of our time.

2. "End Game" Collaboration: A Triple Treat

Taylor Swift's song "End Game" is a special blend of talents. It is featured in her album "Reputation" and brings together Taylor Swift with Ed Sheeran and Future. This unique musical gathering showcases the distinct style of each artist and highlights Taylor's ability to seamlessly merge with artists from various collaboration is a reminder that amazing music often emerges from the fusion of diverse beats and voices.

DID YOU KNOW?

3. Origin of "Swifties": A Fan-Created Phenomenon

The term "Swifties," used to describe the dedicated fans of Taylor Swift, was not a creation of Taylor herself or any official source. Instead, it emerged organically among the fans, primarily on social media platforms. As Taylor's fan community grew and interconnected online, they embraced this nickname as a symbol of their collective admiration and support for Taylor Swift. The evolution of "Swifties" as a term reflects the strong sense of community and passion that characterizes her fan base, highlighting the unique bond shared by fans around the world. 3. Origin of "Swifties": A Fan-Created Phenomenon

4. Taylor Swift's Early Tour Experience with Keith Urban

In 2009, during the early stages of her career, Taylor Swift was chosen to be a supporting act for Keith Urban's Escape Together World Tour. This experience proved to be a significant milestone for Taylor, as it gave her the opportunity to perform in front of large audiences and greatly expand her exposure. Being part of Keith Urban's tour, who was already an established artist, helped cement Taylor's position as an upcoming star in the country music world. This experience was the first step in her journey towards becoming a household name in the music industry.

DID YOU KNOW?

5. Taylor Swift's Theatrical Role in "Bye Bye Birdie"

During her high school years, Taylor Swift demonstrated her diverse talents by participating in a production of the classic play "Bye Bye Birdie." Her involvement in theatrical performances at a young age highlights her early passion for the performing arts beyond just music. By taking part in such plays, Taylor was able to explore and express her artistic abilities, showcasing the breadth of her interest and talent in entertainment from a young age.

6. Acting Range: A Voice for Animation

Taylor Swift showcased a different side of her talents by lending her voice to a character in "The Lorax", a colorful and imaginative animated film based on the beloved book by Dr. Seuss. Her involvement in the movie not only allowed her to explore a new realm of the entertainment industry but also proved her versatility and willingness to try new things. In "The Lorax", Taylor Swift did not just sing beautifully or write heartfelt songs but also brought a character to life with her voice. Her role in the film is a delightful blend of her artistic skills and a classic story, making it a must-watch for both Taylor Swift fans and animated movie lovers.

DID YOU KNOW?

7. Swift Songwriting: "Better Than Revenge" in Record Time

Taylor Swift's songwriting prowess is nothing short of remarkable. In fact, she wrote "Better Than Revenge" in under 30 minutes, showcasing her exceptional speed and talent in songwriting. Her ability to quickly create lyrics and melodies is a testament to her natural aptitude for music composition. Taylor's skill in rapidly transforming her ideas and emotions into songs is part of what makes her a standout artist in the music industry. Her ability to craft engaging and relatable music in a short span of time is evidenced by this feat and many others.

8. Taylor Swift's Charity Concert for Japan's Earthquake and Tsunami Victims

In the aftermath of the devastating earthquake and tsunami that struck Japan in 2011, Taylor Swift organized a charity concert to raise funds for the affected individuals and communities. With her unwavering dedication to humanitarian causes, this act of kindness highlights her commitment to helping those in need. Through this event, Taylor not only collected funds but also drew attention to the crisis and urged others to support relief efforts. Her involvement in this charitable act demonstrates her compassionate nature and willingness to assist communities in distress, further cementing her position as a socially responsible and caring public figure.

DID YOU KNOW?

9. Taylor Swift's Trailblazing Achievement at the MTV VMAs

Taylor Swift made history at the MTV VMAs by becoming the first female solo artist to win two Video of the Year awards for "Bad Blood" and "You Need to Calm Down". This remarkable achievement highlights Taylor's significant influence and impact in the music industry, particularly in the realm of music videos. Her ability to create visually stunning and meaningful videos has not only resonated with audiences but has also been recognized and celebrated within the industry. This milestone is a testament to her creativity and her status in the music world.

10. Secret Collaboration: "This Is What You Came For" with Calvin Harris

Taylor Swift secretly collaborated with Calvin Harris on the hit song "This Is What You Came For". Under the pseudonym Nils Sjöberg, she co-wrote the song with him. This decision to keep the collaboration a secret showcased Taylor's versatility and her willingness to experiment with different aspects of songwriting. By using a pseudonym, she was able to make significant contributions to the song without the immediate influence of her well-known name. This approach demonstrates Taylor's creative approach to music production and her ability to contribute behind the scenes.

DID YOU KNOW?

11. Honorary Doctorate from New York University for Taylor Swift

The term "Swifties," used to describe the dedicated fans of Taylor Swift, was not a creation of Taylor herself or any official source. Instead, it emerged organically among the fans, primarily on social media platforms. As Taylor's fan community grew and interconnected online, they embraced this nickname as a symbol of their collective admiration and support for Taylor Swift. The evolution of "Swifties" as a term reflects the strong sense of community and passion that characterizes her fan base, highlighting the unique bond shared by fans around the world.

12. ·Taylor Swift and the Songwriters Hall of Fame

Taylor Swift, a renowned singer-songwriter, has not been inducted into the Songwriters Hall of Fame as per the latest information. Despite her exceptional songwriting talents and multiple awards, this specific honor has not been bestowed upon her yet. Taylor's emotionally rich and storytelling songs have significantly influenced popular music, but the Songwriters Hall of Fame induction continues to elude her. This fact highlights the exclusive and prestigious nature of recognition in the music industry.

DID YOU KNOW?

13. "Sweeter than Fiction" for "One Chance" Soundtrack

Taylor Swift's contribution of "Sweeter than Fiction" to the soundtrack of the animated movie "One Chance" showcased her ability to create music that is not only powerful on its own but also complements cinematic storytelling. By aligning her songwriting skills with the themes and narratives of the film, Taylor demonstrated her versatility as an artist and her aptitude in crafting songs that resonate with diverse audiences and contexts. Her contribution to "One Chance" is a reflection of her talent in merging music with storytelling across various artistic forms.

14. Taylor Swift as Time's Person of the Year

In 2017, Taylor Swift was recognized by Time magazine as one of the "Persons of the Year". She was honored as part of the "Silence Breakers" group for her contributions to the #MeToo movement and her stance against sexual harassment. This acknowledgment highlights Taylor's influence beyond her music and recognizes her as a significant figure in societal and cultural discussions. Her involvement in the #MeToo movement and her public stance against sexual harassment demonstrate her commitment to using her platform for advocacy and change, making her a prominent voice in important social issues.

DID YOU KNOW?

15. Taylor Swift's National Anthem Performance at a 76ers Game

Taylor Swift's national anthem performance at a 76ers game was a pivotal moment in her early career. It was the first time she captured the public's attention beyond the local stages where she had been performing. Singing at such a high-profile sports event, especially at a young age, was a significant step in her journey towards becoming a well-known artist. Her vocal talent was showcased to a broader audience, and this performance is often remembered as one of the early indicators of her potential to become a star in the music industry.

16. Taylor Swift's Record-Breaking Night at the American Music Awards

Taylor Swift made history at the American Music Awards by winning six awards in one night. Her incredible achievement showcased her immense popularity, critical acclaim, and influential presence in the music industry. Winning such a significant number of awards at a single event not only highlights her talent and the quality of her music but also reflects the strong bond she has with her fans. This milestone in her career serves as a testament to her lasting impact and success as one of the most prominent figures in contemporary music.

DID YOU KNOW?

17. Taylor Swift's Venture into the World of Acting

Taylor Swift has ventured into the world of acting alongside her successful music career. She has appeared in several films, including "Valentine's Day" and "The Giver," and has made guest appearances on various television shows. These acting roles showcase her versatility as an entertainer and her ability to adapt to different forms of media. Taylor's involvement in acting reflects her interest in exploring diverse creative outlets, further highlighting her multifaceted talent and her willingness to expand her artistic horizons beyond music.

18. Heartbeat in "Wildest Dreams"

In her song "Wildest Dreams," Taylor Swift incorporates the sound of a heartbeat as an instrument, showcasing her innovative approach to music production. This unconventional use of a heartbeat as a musical element adds a personal touch to the song, making it more emotionally impactful. Taylor's ability to blend traditional and unique elements in her music is evident in this feature, which highlights her creative skills. Overall, the use of a heartbeat in "Wildest Dreams" demonstrates Taylor's talent in creating unique and relatable songs that appeal to a wide audience.

DID YOU KNOW?

19. Ownership of Masters in "Lover" Album

Taylor Swift's album "Lover," which was released in 2019, marked a significant milestone in her career as it was the first album for which she owned the master recordings outright. This was a clear indication of her efforts to maintain artistic and financial control over her work. By owning the masters to "Lover," Taylor demonstrated her strong commitment to having autonomy over her music and its distribution. This move was widely seen as a powerful statement in the music industry, emphasizing the importance of artists controlling their own creative output and rights.

20. "Safe & Sound" for "The Hunger Games"

"Safe & Sound" was a song co-written and performed by Taylor Swift for the movie soundtrack of "The Hunger Games," which also features The Civil Wars. The song's solemn and haunting atmosphere perfectly resonates with the movie's tone and theme, significantly adding to its narrative. Taylor's ability to craft such a song showcases her remarkable songwriting skills and sensitivity to the art of storytelling through film. "Safe & Sound" is not just a memorable part of "The Hunger Games" soundtrack, but also a prime example of Taylor's talent in merging music with cinematic expression.

DID YOU KNOW?

21. Personal Touch in Taylor Swift's Songwriting

Taylor Swift is known for incorporating narratives about her personal experiences and relationships into her music writing. This unique aspect of her songs has created a profound and authentic connection with her listeners. Taylor's music reflects real emotions and experiences, which resonates with many of her fans, who find similarities in their own lives. Her songwriting approach, characterized by its sincerity and vulnerability, has not only defined her style but also contributed to her widespread popularity. This personal touch in her lyrics is a crucial factor in why Taylor Swift's music is so relatable.

22. "Ronan": A Heartfelt Tribute by Taylor Swift

"Ronan" is a particularly poignant song performed by Taylor Swift. It is dedicated to a young boy named Ronan who passed away from neuroblastoma. Taylor has performed this song live only on rare occasions, making it a deeply moving and memorable part of her repertoire. The song's heartfelt and emotional lyrics showcase Taylor's ability to convey deep empathy and compassion through her music. Her tribute in "Ronan" not only honors the memory of the young boy but also touches on the universal themes of loss and love, resonating deeply with listeners who have experienced similar sorrows.

DID YOU KNOW?

23. "Fearless": Taylor Swift's Grammy Milestone

In 2010, Taylor Swift's album "Fearless" won the Grammy Award for Album of the Year, a significant milestone in her career. This win made her the youngest artist to receive this honor at the time. "Fearless" included popular hits like "Love Story" and "You Belong With Me," which helped establish Taylor's status as a crossover sensation in the music industry. This Grammy win was not only a testament to the album's success and appeal but also marked a crucial moment in Taylor's career, highlighting her talents as a songwriter and her appeal across various music genres.

24. Exploring Beyond Country and Pop: Taylor Swift's Musical Range

It is a common misconception that Taylor Swift has only released albums in the country and pop genres. However, throughout her career, Taylor has continuously explored and embraced a variety of musical styles. Albums such as "Folklore" and "Evermore" are excellent examples of her musical range, as they delve into indie folk, alternative rock, and electro-folk genres. This exploration showcases Taylor's versatility as an artist and her willingness to experiment with different sounds and themes.

Test
Your Knowledge!

What creative hobby does Taylor Swift enjoy when she's not writing songs or performing?

A) Cooking
B) Painting
C) Gardening
D) All of the above

Which prestigious music award has Taylor Swift won multiple times?

A) MTV Video Music Award
B) Billboard Music Award
C) Grammy Award for Album of the Year
D) American Music Award for Artist of the Year

Answers

What creative hobby does Taylor Swift enjoy when she's not writing songs or performing?

A) Cooking
B) Painting
C) Gardening
D) All of the above

Which prestigious music award has Taylor Swift won multiple times?

A) MTV Video Music Award
B) Billboard Music Award
C) Grammy Award for Album of the Year
D) American Music Award for Artist of the Year

DID YOU KNOW?

25. Shania Twain: A Key Influence on Taylor Swift

Shania Twain has been a key influence on Taylor Swift's music career. Taylor has repeatedly credited Shania as a major inspiration for her decision to pursue country music. Shania Twain's success in the crossover into pop music had a significant impact on Taylor, motivating her to blend different genres in her own music career. This influence is noticeable in Taylor's songwriting approach and her ability to appeal to audiences from both country and pop music. Shania Twain's example demonstrated to Taylor the potential of blending genres and assisted her in shaping her path as an artist who transcends traditional musical boundaries.

26. Taylor Swift's Contributions to Education

Taylor Swift has made significant contributions to education by donating funds to support schools and public libraries. Her generous donations reflect her strong commitment to literacy and learning. Taylor's involvement in educational initiatives highlights her understanding of the importance of education and her desire to give back to the community in meaningful ways. In addition to her financial contributions, she also raises awareness about the significance of education and the need for resources in schools and libraries, proving her dedication to making a positive impact in this area.

DID YOU KNOW?

27. Taylor Swift's Unique Snow Globe Collection

Taylor Swift has a charming and unusual hobby of collecting snow globes that she has mentioned in various interviews. This unique collection reflects a personal and whimsical aspect of her public persona. Snow globes have miniature scenes that offer a magical quality of snowfall at the shake of a hand, reflecting a sense of wonder and nostalgia. These qualities are often found in Taylor's music and public image. This hobby provides a glimpse into the more personal and playful side of Taylor Swift, which goes beyond her music and public life.

28. Taylor Swift's Support for Environmental Causes

Taylor Swift is an active supporter of environmental causes and sustainability. Her advocacy in this area reflects her commitment to raising awareness and encouraging action to protect the environment. By getting involved in environmental issues, Taylor demonstrates her understanding of the importance of these causes and her willingness to use her platform to promote positive change. Her support for sustainability and environmental protection aligns with a growing movement in the entertainment industry towards greater ecological responsibility and conscious living.

DID YOU KNOW?

29. Taylor Swift's Bold and Eclectic Fashion Style

Taylor Swift's fashion style is best described as unique and daring, which is a reflection of her personality and her approach to self-expression. Her willingness to experiment with different looks showcases her eclectic fashion sense, blending various fashion elements to create outfits that are striking and one-of-a-kind. Similar to her music, Taylor's fashion choices reflect her creativity and versatility, where she combines diverse influences to craft something that is distinctly her own. Her bold fashion choices often make a statement, highlighting her confidence, individuality, and her ability to push boundaries.

30. Taylor Swift's Language Proficiency

t's a common misconception that Taylor Swift is fluent in multiple languages. Although she has expressed interest in learning other languages, there is no evidence to suggest that she is proficient in any language other than English. Taylor's eagerness to learn new languages reflects her curiosity and passion for connecting with diverse cultures, but according to the latest information available, she hasn't achieved fluency in any language. However, her interest in learning languages highlights her openness to embracing diverse cultural experiences and her global perspective as an artist.

DID YOU KNOW?

31. Taylor Swift's Favorite Number: 13

Taylor Swift's favorite number is 13. She considers it her lucky number and often incorporates it into her music and personal life. The number 13 has become a signature element for Taylor, reflecting her belief in its luck and significance. This preference for the number 13 is just one of the many personal touches that Taylor brings to her work, creating a unique connection with her fans who have come to recognize and appreciate these personal symbols in her music and public appearances.

32. Taylor Swift and Her Brother in the Entertainment Industry

Taylor Swift has a brother named Austin Swift, who is also a part of the entertainment industry as an actor. Therefore, the Swift family shares a common interest in creative expression. Taylor's successful career in music and Austin's involvement in acting illustrate the diverse artistic pursuits of the siblings.

DID YOU KNOW?

33. Discovery of Taylor Swift by Scott Borchetta

Scott Borchetta, a music manager, is credited with discovering Taylor Swift during one of her performances at The Bluebird Café in Nashville. This encounter with Borchetta was a pivotal moment in Taylor's career, as it resulted in her first record deal and set the stage for her rise to stardom. Borchetta's recognition of Taylor's talent during that café performance was instrumental in launching her into the music industry, where she went on to achieve widespread acclaim and success. This moment at The Bluebird Café is often looked back on as a defining starting point in Taylor Swift's journey as a prominent artist.

34. Taylor Swift's Close-Knit Circle of Celebrity Friends

Taylor Swift is well-known for maintaining close friendships with many high-profile celebrities. Her circle of famous friends includes notable figures from the entertainment industry, highlighting her value for deep and lasting relationships. These friendships are often in the public eye and demonstrate her commitment to maintaining personal connections despite her fame and busy career. The friendships she has forged with other celebrities are a notable aspect of her public persona, showcasing her ability to develop and maintain meaningful relationships in the often-transient world of show business.

DID YOU KNOW?

35. Taylor Swift's Favorite School Subject: English

During her school years, Taylor Swift's favorite subject was English. This fondness for the subject is not surprising, given her passion for storytelling and songwriting. The English curriculum typically includes creative writing, literature, and text analysis, all of which can help develop skills that are essential for a songwriter. Taylor's love for English likely played a crucial role in honing her abilities to craft narrative-driven music and compose lyrics that are both compelling and impactful. Thus, her interest in English serves as an early testament to her talent and inclination towards creating stories through music.

36. Taylor Swift's Passion for Horseback Riding

Taylor Swift has had a love for horses since she was young and used to compete as a teenager. Prior to her rise to fame in the music industry, she was an avid horseback rider and took part in equestrian events. This aspect of her life highlights her varied range of interests and talents from a young age. Her experience in horseback riding is a reflection of her personality and background, which contributed to her overall development as an artist and an individual with a diverse set of passions and experiences.

DID YOU KNOW?

37. Taylor Swift's Initial Interest in Journalism

Prior to pursuing a career in music, Taylor Swift considered journalism as a potential career path. Her interest in journalism reflects her innate passion for writing and storytelling, skills that later became central to her songwriting and overall artistry. This inclination towards journalism highlights her curiosity and desire to explore and comprehend the world around her, traits that have significantly influenced her lyrical style and narrative approach in music. Ultimately, Taylor's decision to focus on music allowed her to channel these storytelling abilities into her songs, forging a deep and resonant connection with her audience.

38. Taylor Swift's Interest in Painting and Visual Arts

Taylor Swift is not only passionate about her music career but also about painting and visual arts. She has expressed her interest in these creative fields and engages in them as a hobby. This aspect of her personality showcases her multifaceted creative talents and her appreciation for diverse forms of artistic expression. Taylor's involvement in painting and visual arts provides her with an alternative avenue for creativity and personal expression, supplementing her primary career as a musician and songwriter. Her interest in these areas demonstrates the breadth of her artistic curiosity and her desire to explore various modes of creative expression.

Test
Your Knowledge!

Which of the following awards has Taylor Swift NOT won?

A) American Music Awards

B) MTV Video Music Awards

C) Billboard Music Awards

D) The Nobel Prize in Literature

Question about Taylor Swift's Guinness World Record: For what achievement did Taylor Swift earn a Guinness World Record in 2018?

A) fastest-selling album release

B) most streamed song in a single day

C) highest-attended U.S. tour by a female artist

D) most followers on Instagram

Answers

Which of the following awards has Taylor
Swift NOT won?

A) American Music Awards

B) MTV Video Music Awards

C) Billboard Music Awards

D) The Nobel Prize in Literature

Question about Taylor Swift's Guinness World
Record: For what achievement did Taylor Swift
earn a Guinness World Record in 2018?

A) fastest-selling album release

B) most streamed song in a single day

**C) highest-attended U.S. tour by a female
artist**

D) most followers on Instagram

DID YOU KNOW?

39. Taylor Swift's Favorite Holiday: Fourth of July

Taylor Swift holds a special place in her heart for the Fourth of July, which happens to be her favorite holiday. She is renowned for her elaborate celebrations of this occasion, often hosting themed parties with her friends and going all out with decorations. These lively gatherings have become somewhat of a tradition and are well-known among her fans. Taylor's enthusiasm for the Fourth of July reflects her love for creating memorable experiences and celebrating special occasions with those close to her. Her grand celebrations on this holiday also showcase her flair for entertaining and her enjoyment of American traditions.

40. Taylor Swift's Philanthropic Efforts and Anonymous Donations

Taylor Swift is known for her philanthropic efforts and generosity towards various charities and people in need. She has made significant donations to support causes that are close to her heart, and often does so anonymously, without seeking any recognition or praise. This selfless approach is a testament to her sincere desire to help those in need, and her actions have been widely appreciated and recognized by the public and recipients alike. Taylor's dedication to making a positive impact on people's lives through her resources and influence is truly commendable.

DID YOU KNOW?

41· Taylor Swift's Preferred Driving Music: Hip-Hop

Taylor Swift has expressed in interviews that her preferred genre of music to listen to while driving is hip-hop· This choice for road trip tunes indicates her diverse taste in music and her appreciation for different genres beyond the ones she typically performs· Hip-hop, known for its rhythmic and lyrical dynamism, offers a different kind of auditory experience that Taylor enjoys, particularly during car trips· Her preference for hip-hop music while driving showcases another facet of her musical interests and her enjoyment of the energy and beats that this genre offers·

42· Taylor Swift's Favorite Food: Cheesecake

Cheesecake happens to be one of Taylor Swift's favorite foods, and she has mentioned it in multiple interviews· Her love for this dessert highlights a relatable and unpretentious aspect of her personality, allowing her to connect with fans over a shared fondness for a popular and classic dessert· Swift's preference for cheesecake contributes to the numerous personal details she shares with her audience, contributing to her approachable and authentic public image·

DID YOU KNOW?

43. Taylor Swift's Love for Reading and Literary Inspiration

Taylor Swift is a voracious reader who often draws inspiration from literature for her music. She is well-known for her love of reading and frequently references literary works and authors in her songs. This aspect of her songwriting reflects her deep appreciation for storytelling and the written word. By incorporating literary elements and themes into her songs, Taylor not only enriches her music but also pays homage to the authors and works that have inspired her. Her ability to weave literary references into her song lyrics is a testament to her creativity and her connection to the broader world of storytelling and art.

44. Taylor Swift's Childhood on a Christmas Tree Farm

Taylor Swift spent her childhood helping out on her family's Christmas tree farm in Pennsylvania. This unique upbringing played a significant role in shaping her personality and work ethic, contributing to her down-to-earth persona. Growing up in such a setting likely instilled in her a strong connection to nature, an appreciation for hard work, and family values, all of which have subtly influenced her music and public image. Her experience on the Christmas tree farm continues to be a noteworthy and frequently cited part of her early life story.

DID YOU KNOW?

45. Taylor Swift's Love for Baking

Taylor Swift has a passion for baking and she enjoys sharing her homemade treats with her friends and family. She is known for her love of baking and often delights in creating cookies, cakes, and other baked goods for her loved ones. This hobby showcases Taylor's personal and nurturing side, reflecting her enjoyment of homey, comforting activities. Her passion for baking and sharing her creations with her loved ones is a testament to her warmth and generosity, adding another layer to her multifaceted personality beyond her successful music career.

46. Taylor Swift's Love for Her Pets!

Taylor Swift is known for her love of cats, and one of her famous feline pets is named Olivia Benson. The cat is named after the character from the TV show "Law & Order: SVU." Olivia Benson, the cat, has gained her own celebrity status, often appearing in Taylor's social media posts and making occasional appearances in her music videos. By naming her cat after a strong and iconic TV character, Taylor showcases her admiration for powerful female figures. Olivia Benson's presence in Taylor's life adds a charming and relatable aspect to her public persona, highlighting her love for her pets and their significance in her life.

DID YOU KNOW?

47. Mark Twain's Influence on Taylor Swift's Storytelling

Taylor Swift has acknowledged Mark Twain's significant influence on her storytelling style in songwriting. Mark Twain, renowned for his wit, humor, and sharp observation of American life, has inspired Taylor in her approach to crafting narratives in her songs. Her admiration for Twain's work reflects Taylor's appreciation for classic American literature and her desire to incorporate similar storytelling techniques into her music. Taylor's ability to weave stories that resonate with listeners, similar to Twain's enduring tales, highlights the impact of literary figures on her artistic development. This literary influence is a testament to the depth and thoughtfulness behind Taylor Swift's songwriting process.

48. Context of Taylor Swift's Quote on Kindness

During a magazine interview, Taylor Swift shared an inspirational quote that reflects her personal philosophy and approach to life. The quote states, "No matter what happens in life, be good to people. Being good to people is a wonderful legacy to leave behind." This quote highlights the importance of kindness and the impact of how we treat others. By sharing this sentiment, Taylor emphasizes her desire to use her platform to promote positive values and attitudes. Many fans have resonated with this quote, which is reflective of the thoughtful and compassionate aspects of her public persona.

DID YOU KNOW?

49. Taylor Swift's Recognition by the Nashville Songwriters Association International

Taylor Swift has been awarded the Songwriter/ Artist of the Year by the Nashville Songwriters Association International more times than any other artist. This achievement is a testament to her remarkable contributions to songwriting and her profound impact on the music industry, especially in the country and pop genres. Taylor is an exceptional songwriter who consistently creates music that resonates with a wide audience. Her repeated recognition by the respected organization highlights her talent, dedication, and influence as both a songwriter and a performing artist.

50. "Fifteen" at the 2010 Grammy Awards: A Career Milestone for Taylor Swift

In 2010, Taylor Swift performed "Fifteen" at the Grammy Awards, which was a significant event in her early career. This performance highlighted her rising status in the music industry and showcased her talent on one of its most prestigious stages. The choice of "Fifteen," a song that resonates with themes of youth and experiences of growing up, allowed Taylor to deeply connect with a diverse audience and further establish herself as a relatable and influential artist. Her performance at the Grammy Awards was not just a showcase of her musical talent, but also a reflection of her ability to capture and express universal emotions through her music.

Test
Your Knowledge!

How has Taylor Swift shown her commitment to her hometown in Pennsylvania?

A) By hosting annual concerts in the town

B) By donating to local schools and charities

C) By establishing a music festival in her name

D) By building a performing arts center

Where can you find a dedicated exhibit celebrating Taylor Swift's influence in music and pop culture?

A) The Metropolitan Museum of Art

B) The Smithsonian Institution

C) The Grammy Museum

D) The Louvre Museum

Answers

How has Taylor Swift shown her commitment to her hometown in Pennsylvania?

A) By hosting annual concerts in the town
B) By donating to local schools and charities
C) By establishing a music festival in her name
D) By building a performing arts center

Where can you find a dedicated exhibit celebrating Taylor Swift's influence in music and pop culture?

A) The Metropolitan Museum of Art
B) The Smithsonian Institution
C) The Grammy Museum
D) The Louvre Museum

DID YOU KNOW?

51. Taylor Swift's Exploration of Various Music Genres

It is true that Taylor Swift has experimented with genres outside of country and pop, including rock and electronic music. Throughout her career, Taylor has showcased her versatility as an artist by exploring different musical styles. Her forays into rock and electronic music demonstrate her willingness to push the boundaries of her sound and to continually evolve as a musician. This exploration into various genres not only highlights her adaptability but also her desire to experiment and challenge herself artistically. Taylor's ability to successfully navigate through different musical landscapes is a testament to her talent and her broad appeal as a contemporary artist.

52. Taylor Swift's Childhood Passion for Creative Writing

Taylor Swift had a strong passion for creative writing during her childhood. She frequently wrote poems and stories, which greatly contributed to her exceptional songwriting skills. Her interest in creative writing from a young age established the foundation for her narrative approach to songwriting. This enabled her to create emotionally resonant lyrics with vivid imagery, which is evident in her music. Taylor's childhood hobby has significantly influenced her artistic career.

DID YOU KNOW?

53. Taylor Swift's Early Tour Experience with Rascal Flatts

In the early days of her career as a country music artist, Taylor Swift opened for Rascal Flatts on their tour. This opportunity provided her with significant exposure and experience in the country music scene. Being a supporting act for a well-established group like Rascal Flatts allowed Taylor to perform in front of large audiences, helping to build her fan base and gain invaluable stage experience. This period in her career was crucial for her development as a performer and played a key role in her journey towards becoming a prominent figure in country music and later in the broader music industry.

54. Reference to "Pride and Prejudice" in Taylor Swift's "Love Story"

Taylor Swift's song "Love Story" includes a reference to Jane Austen's classic novel "Pride and Prejudice." In the song, Taylor compares the storyline of her song to the classic love story depicted in the novel. This reference adds a unique and captivating element to "Love Story" as it blends modern storytelling with the elements of literary classics. Taylor's ability to incorporate a literary reference in her music portrays her creative talent in combining different artistic influences to create deeply personal and relatable songs.

DID YOU KNOW?

55. Taylor Swift's Directorial Achievement with "Cardigan"

At the MTV Video Music Awards, Taylor Swift's music video for "Cardigan" won the Best Direction award, which is an impressive feat. This achievement not only recognizes Taylor as a talented musician but also as a skilled music video director. With her exceptional artistic vision and storytelling skills, Taylor brought her creative ideas to life in "Cardigan," making it a visually stunning music video. Winning this award for a video she directed herself is a significant milestone in her career, demonstrating her diverse talents and her ability to excel in various aspects of the music industry.

56. Taylor Swift's Record Label Transition

It is false that Taylor Swift created her own record label to release her future albums. While she has been very proactive about her music rights, Taylor did not establish her own label. Instead, she made a significant move by signing with Republic Records after leaving Big Machine Records. This transition was a notable moment in her career, reflecting her desire for greater control over her music and her future projects. Her decision to join Republic Records highlights her strategic approach to managing her career and maintaining artistic freedom in the music industry.

DID YOU KNOW?

57. Taylor Swift's '1989' Surpasses 6 Million U.S. Sales, Securing Multi-Platinum Triumph

Taylor Swift is a record-breaking musician who has achieved numerous Gold and Platinum certifications for her albums and singles. One of her notable accomplishments is her 2014 album "1989," which won the Grammy Award for Album of the Year and achieved multi-Platinum status by selling over 6 million copies in the U.S. alone. The album features hits like "Shake It Off" and "Blank Space," which have contributed to Taylor Swift's widespread appeal and enduring impact in the music industry. Her consistent ability to achieve high sales and earn prestigious music plaques across multiple albums is a testament to both her artistic talent and her Global connection.

58. Collaboration with Bon Iver on "Evermore"

Taylor Swift collaborated with the legendary folk artist Bon Iver on her album "Evermore." The song "Exile," featuring Bon Iver, is a standout track from this album, known for its haunting and emotive duet. This collaboration showcases Taylor Swift's versatility and her ability to blend her style with artists from different genres. The pairing of their distinct voices in "Exile" creates a deeply resonant and powerful musical experience, highlighting the strengths of both artists. This song has been widely praised and is a testament to Taylor's continual evolution as a musician and artist.

DID YOU KNOW?

59. Taylor Swift's Advocacy on Multiple Political Issues

Taylor Swift has been a vocal advocate for various political issues ranging from climate change, LGBTQ+ rights, and education reform. Her advocacy efforts demonstrate her commitment to social and political activism, utilizing her platform to bring attention to critical issues. In recent years, she has been particularly outspoken and used her influence to promote LGBTQ+ rights, call for action on climate change, and support education reform. Taylor's involvement in these matters highlights her role as an artist who is deeply concerned about global societal issues and is dedicated to making a positive impact beyond her music career.

60. Taylor Swift's Role as a Music Video Director

Taylor Swift has proven herself to be a multi-talented artist by directing some of her own music videos. This additional role allows her to showcase her creative vision and artistic control beyond her skills as a musician and songwriter. By directing her own music videos, Taylor is able to convey her artistic

DID YOU KNOW?

61. Taylor Swift's First World Tour: The Fearless

The name of Taylor Swift's first world tour was The Fearless Tour. This tour was in support of her album "Fearless" and marked her first venture as a headlining artist on a global scale. The Fearless Tour showcased Taylor Swift's rise as a global star in the music industry, demonstrating her widespread appeal and her ability to captivate audiences around the world. This tour was a significant step in her career, solidifying her status as a leading figure in the music scene and highlighting her talents as a live performer.

62. Taylor Swift's Record-Breaking Achievement with "Fearless"

Taylor Swift has achieved a record-breaking milestone with her album "Fearless". She is the only female artist in the 21st century to have her album on the Billboard 200 chart for 400 weeks. This achievement speaks volumes about Taylor's enduring popularity and her impact on the music

DID YOU KNOW?

63. Faith Hill's Mentorship to Taylor Swift

During the initial stages of her career in country music, Taylor Swift was fortunate to have Faith Hill as her early mentor. Faith Hill, an established star in the country music scene, offered valuable guidance and insights to help Taylor navigate the challenges and opportunities of the music industry. This mentorship highlights the supportive nature of the country music community and the importance of established artists investing in emerging talent. Taylor's relationship with Faith Hill is a testimony to the significance of early connections in the industry and the role these relationships played in her development as an artist.

64. First Record Deal at Age 15

Taylor Swift's journey as a music artist started at a very young age. She signed her first record deal with Big Machine Records when she was just 15 years old. This early exposure to the music industry paved the way for her future success as a global music sensation. The fact that she was signed at such a young age is a testament to her early talent and the potential that Big Machine Records saw in her as a future star.

Test
Your Knowledge!

How has Taylor Swift used her platform in relation to social issues?

A) By promoting her own fashion line

B) By speaking out against injustice and promoting equality

C) By endorsing political candidates

D) By focusing solely on music and avoiding social topics

What personal interest of Taylor Swift often influences her music and personal life?

A) Her love for the outdoors and natural world

B) Her passion for cooking and baking

C) Her interest in vintage fashion

D) Her hobby of collecting rare books

Answers

How has Taylor Swift used her platform in relation to social issues?

A) By promoting her own fashion line

B) By speaking out against injustice and promoting equality

C) By endorsing political candidates

D) By focusing solely on music and avoiding social topics

What personal interest of Taylor Swift often influences her music and personal life?

A) Her love for the outdoors and natural world

B) Her passion for cooking and baking

C) Her interest in vintage fashion

D) Her hobby of collecting rare books

DID YOU KNOW?

65. Secret Messages in Album Booklets

Taylor Swift is known for including secret messages in the lyrics of her album booklets. Her unique and personal songwriting style is enhanced by these hidden messages, which add an additional layer of meaning to her songs. These messages often provide insights into her thoughts, experiences, and the stories behind her music, and have become a hallmark of her albums. Fans enjoy deciphering the messages, which help them gain a better understanding of her music and create a deeper connection with her.

66. "The Man" by Taylor Swift: A Commentary on Gender Inequality

Taylor Swift's song "The Man" delves into the themes of gender inequality and double standards prevalent in our society. The song addresses the disparities and biases that women face, particularly in the context of success and leadership. Through her music, Taylor uses her platform to comment on social issues and highlights her ability to weave them into her songwriting. "The Man" is a reflection of her commitment to use her voice and influence to address significant social issues. The song not only entertains but also prompts its listeners to think critically about the gender dynamics in contemporary society.

DID YOU KNOW?

67. Taylor Swift's Record-Breaking Achievement with "Reputation"

Taylor Swift's album "Reputation" marked a significant achievement in her career. She became the first female artist to have six consecutive albums, each selling over a million copies in their first week. This milestone underscores Taylor Swift's immense popularity and the strong demand for her music. Her ability to consistently achieve high sales with multiple albums reflects her enduring appeal and the deep connection she has established with her audience. This record-breaking feat with "Reputation" highlights Taylor's status as one of the most influential and successful artists in the contemporary music.

68. Taylor Swift's Philanthropic Response to COVID-19 Pandemic

Taylor Swift showed her philanthropic side by providing financial aid to her fans who were facing financial difficulties. Her decision to assist her fans directly is a testament to her empathy and the strong bond she shares with her fanbase. Acknowledging the challenges that arose during the pandemic, Taylor's personal contributions reflect her commitment to giving back and supporting her community in times of need. Her act of helping fans in a state of financial distress exemplifies her compassion and willingness to utilize her resources to make a positive impact on people's lives.

DID YOU KNOW?

69. Influence of Shakespeare in Taylor Swift's "Love Story"

Taylor Swift's seventh studio album, released in 2019, is entitled "Lover." This album marks a clear departure from the darker themes and tones of her previous album, "Reputation," and features a brighter, more romantic aesthetic. It showcases Taylor's musical versatility, with a mix of upbeat pop songs and heartfelt ballads. The album has been praised for its lyrical depth, musical diversity, and personal touch, all of which demonstrate Taylor's evolution as an artist. With "Lover," Taylor has shown that she can explore new styles and themes while staying true to her signature sound.

70. Title of Taylor Swift's Seventh Studio Album: "Lover"

Taylor Swift made her acting debut in the television series "CSI: Crime Scene Investigation" in 2009. Her performance in this show was her first attempt at acting, showcasing her abilities beyond her established career in music. Taylor's role in "CSI" allowed her to demonstrate her versatility as a performer and her willingness to take on new challenges in different areas of the entertainment industry. This appearance was one of the early indicators of Taylor's interest in exploring various aspects of creative expression beyond singing and songwriting. Her acting debut in "CSI" is widely remembered.

DID YOU KNOW?

74. "Christmas Tree Farm" by Taylor Swift

Taylor Swift has a Christmas song called "Christmas Tree Farm." The song is based on her childhood experiences and draws inspiration from her memories of growing up on a Christmas tree farm. In "Christmas Tree Farm," Taylor Swift reflects on her own past and the joys of the holiday season, adding a personal and nostalgic element to her music. The song not only contributes to the festive music repertoire but also offers a glimpse into Taylor's upbringing and the experiences that have shaped her. Her songwriting skills are evidenced by her ability to transform personal memories into a universally relatable song.

75. Dazzling Designs: The Fashion Magic of Taylor Swift's Eras Tour"

Taylor Swift's Eras Tour fashion was a huge project. She worked with top designers to make her music look as good as it sounds. Some outfits took over 350 hours to make by hand, showing how much detail goes into each one, just like in Taylor's shows. The tour's clothes, which included special and famous pieces, got lots of compliments. Even The New York Times said it was like a groundbreaking fashion show, changing the game for what people wear at concerts.

DID YOU KNOW?

75. Taylor Swift's Re-recording of Albums

Taylor Swift, the famous singer, has begun the process of re-recording her older albums to regain control over her masters. This decision was made in response to the sale of her original recordings' masters, over which she had no control. "Fearless (Taylor's Version)" was Taylor Swift's first re-recorded album, and it is part of her larger effort to own the rights to her music. By re-recording her earlier albums, Taylor not only reclaims control over her work but also provides her fans with new versions of their favorite songs. Her move has been widely praised as a strong statement about the importance of artists' rights and control over their own creations in the music industry.

76. Taylor Swift's Signature Instrument: Guitar

Taylor Swift is widely recognized for her guitar playing skills, which she often showcases in her performances, concerts, and music videos. The guitar has been a crucial instrument in Taylor's career and has accompanied her in acoustic performances and songwriting sessions. Her ability to play the guitar has not only added to her versatility as a musician but has also connected her to the traditions of the country and singer-songwriter genres. It has become one of her trademarks, highlighting her musical talent and personal style.

DID YOU KNOW?

77. Taylor Swift's Hometown: Reading, Pennsylvania

Taylor Swift's hometown is Reading, Pennsylvania, where she was born and raised before moving to Nashville, Tennessee, to pursue her music career. Her upbringing in Reading played a vital role in her early life and development as an artist. Moving to Nashville was a pivotal step in her journey to becoming a successful musician, considering the city's rich music scene, particularly for country music. Taylor Swift's roots in Reading, Pennsylvania, have contributed to her distinct identity as an artist.

78. Taylor Swift's Unique Zoological Honor

Taylor Swift has been honored with a unique zoological tribute. A species of millipede discovered in Tennessee has been named Nannaria swiftae in recognition of her influence beyond the music industry. Scientists often name species after famous people to acknowledge their contributions to culture and society. Taylor Swift's recognition as a cultural icon is reflected in the naming of Nannaria swiftae, which also celebrates her connection to the state of Tennessee, where she began her music career.

Test
Your Knowledge!

What was Taylor Swift's first job in the music industry?

A) A backup singer for other artists

B) Working at a record label's marketing department

C) Assisting with demo tapes at a recording studio

D) A songwriter for other musicians

Which season does Taylor Swift particularly adore and often celebrates in her music and decorations?

A) Summer

B) Spring

C) Autumn

D) Winter

Answers

What was Taylor Swift's first job in
the music industry?

A) A backup singer for other artists

B) Working at a record label's marketing
department

**C) Assisting with demo tapes at a recording
studio**

D) A songwriter for other musicians

Which season does Taylor Swift particularly
adore and often celebrates in her music and
decorations?

A) Summer

B) Spring

C) Autumn

D) Winter because its Christmas!

DID YOU KNOW?

79. Taylor Swift's Childhood Dream of Becoming a Novelist

In her childhood, before pursuing a career in music, Taylor Swift's dream was to become a novelist. Her love for storytelling and writing as a child laid the groundwork for her lyrical style, characterized by emotional depth and vivid storytelling. Her early ambition to become a novelist demonstrates her creative spirit and her passion for expressing herself through words, which she has successfully carried over into her songwriting career. Taylor Swift's musical style has undergone a significant change with her album "Folklore" released in 2020.

80. Taylor Swift's Genre Shift with "Folklore"

It was the first time she had explored the indie folk genre. The album showcased her versatility and ability to evolve as an artist, featuring a more subdued, introspective and narrative-driven approach, diverging from the more mainstream pop sound of her previous albums. Its lyrical depth and mature, thoughtful music earned it critical acclaim, further solidifying her reputation as an innovative musician capable of crossing genre boundaries.

DID YOU KNOW?

81. Taylor Swift's Record-Breaking Grammy Win at Age 20

At the young age of 20, Taylor Swift became the youngest-ever recipient of the Grammy Award for Album of the Year, thanks to her album "Fearless." Winning the Album of the Year Grammy at such an early age was a significant achievement for her career, highlighting her exceptional talent as a musician and songwriter. This accolade set a record at the time and confirmed her status as a major artist early in her career. "Fearless" not only enjoyed commercial success but also garnered critical acclaim, reflecting the widespread appeal and artistic quality of Taylor's work.

82. Joni Mitchell's Influence on Taylor Swift

Taylor Swift has named Joni Mitchell as a significant influence on her songwriting style and artistic expression. It is particularly evident in Taylor's narrative lyricism, a style for which Joni Mitchell is renowned. Mitchell is known for her poignant storytelling and emotional depth in her songs, which has inspired Taylor Swift to adopt a similar approach in her own music. The influence of Joni Mitchell on Taylor Swift underscores the continuity and evolution of songwriting across different eras in music history, with Taylor adapting and extending the legacy of narrative-driven, deeply personal songwriting.

DID YOU KNOW?

83. Taylor Swift's Songwriting Accomplishments

It is undoubtedly true that Taylor Swift wrote or co-wrote every song in her discography. This fact is a testament to her songwriting skills and artistic authenticity. Taylor's involvement in the writing process of her music has been a defining feature of her career, showcasing her ability to craft deeply personal and relatable songs. As a songwriter, she highlights not only her talent but also her desire to maintain a personal connection with her music. This ensures that each song reflects her own experiences, emotions, and artistic vision. Her dedication to writing her own music has significantly contributed to Taylor Swift's success and reputation as one of the most respected and influential artists.

84. Time-Traveling Tunes: The Epic Journey of Taylor Swift's Eras Tour

Taylor Swift's Eras Tour is like traveling through time in music, lasting more than three hours and 15 minutes, making it her longest concert ever! The show features 44 songs divided into 10 acts, with each section feeling like a different part of Taylor's musical history. Picture a concert where every song brings a new color and style – from the soft, dreamy shades of 'Lover' to the enchanting forest feel of 'Evermore' and the strong, striking atmosphere of 'Reputation.'

DID YOU KNOW?

85. Record-Breaker: Taylor Swift's Historic Triumph at the American Music Awards

At the American Music Awards, Taylor Swift made history by becoming the female artist with the most wins ever, highlighting her enduring popularity and influence in the music industry. This remarkable achievement, along with her expanding array of AMAs, underscores her status as a prominent figure in the current music scene, where she is widely celebrated and recognized for her musical skills and accomplishments.

86. Taylor Swift's Unprecedented Billboard Achievement

Taylor Swift holds the unique distinction of being the only artist to have won the Billboard Woman of the Year award three times. This exceptional accomplishment underscores her extraordinary influence and impact in the music industry. Being recognized as Billboard Woman of the Year multiple times reflects not only Taylor Swift's commercial success but also her significant contributions to the music industry, her role in shaping contemporary music, and her influence as a cultural icon. This honor acknowledges her continuous evolution as an artist, her leadership qualities, and her ability to inspire and empower through her music and public persona. Taylor's repeated recognition in this category highlights her enduring presence and significance in the music world.

DID YOU KNOW?

87. Taylor Swift's Prolific Songwriting: Number of Released Songs

Taylor Swift has released over 150 songs until April 2023, which includes tracks from her studio albums, extended plays, and singles, as well as re-recorded versions and bonus tracks. Her extensive discography showcases her prolific nature as a songwriter and artist, consistently producing music that resonates with a wide audience. Her ability to write and release a large number of songs over the years is a testament to her creativity, work ethic, and enduring popularity in the music industry.

88. Taylor Swift's Record Label Transition

Contrary to popular belief, Taylor Swift has not always been signed to the same record label throughout her career. She kickstarted her career with Big Machine Records, where she achieved tremendous success and released several albums. However, in 2018, Taylor Swift made a significant change by signing with Republic Records. This move marked a pivotal moment in her career, signifying a new phase in her music journey and her eagerness for different opportunities and experiences within the industry. The transition to Republic Records represented a shift in Taylor's professional relationships and business strategy, reflecting her evolving position as a leading figure in the music world.

DID YOU KNOW?

89. Inspiration Behind "Style"

"Style" is widely believed to be a Taylor Swift song inspired by her relationship with Harry Styles, a member of the boy band One Direction. The song's title itself is often seen as a nod to Styles' last name, and the lyrics contain references that fans and listeners have connected to their brief relationship. This connection adds a layer of personal context to the song, which is known for its catchy melody and reflective lyrics on a past romance. "Style" is a prime example of how her personal life has influenced her music, resonating with audiences who find common ground in the themes of love and relationships.

90. Release of "1989" Featuring "Shake It Off"

Taylor Swift is known for supporting various causes, including animal rights, education and literacy, and disaster relief. Her involvement in these charitable efforts showcases her commitment to giving back to the community and using her platform for positive impact. Taylor's support for animal rights reflects her compassion for living beings, while her contributions to education and literacy highlight her belief in the power of knowledge and learning. Her involvement in disaster relief efforts demonstrates her responsiveness to immediate global needs and crises. Taylor Swift's broad philanthropic work illustrates her dedication to addressing a range of important social issues,

DID YOU KNOW?

91. Taylor Swift's Diverse Charitable Involvement

In 2014, Taylor Swift released the album "1989," featuring the popular single "Shake It Off." This album marked a significant shift in her music style, transitioning from country to pop. The album was a commercial and critical success, with "Shake It Off" becoming one of its most recognizable and popular tracks. The album showcased Taylor's versatility as an artist, successfully navigating different musical genres. It played a pivotal role in redefining her career and solidifying her status as a pop music icon.

92. Taylor Swift's Early Songwriting Talent

The song "Style" is believed to have been inspired by Taylor Swift's relationship with Harry Styles, a member of the boy band One Direction. The song's title is often seen as a nod to Styles' last name, and the lyrics contain references that fans and listeners have connected to their brief relationship. This connection adds a personal context to the song, which is known for its catchy melody and reflective lyrics on a past romance. Taylor Swift's ability to draw from personal experiences and transform them into relatable music has been a hallmark of her songwriting throughout her career. "Style" is a prime example of how her personal life has influenced her music, resonating with audiences who find common ground in the themes of love and relationships.

Test
Your Knowledge!

What aspect of global diversity has Taylor Swift shown a keen interest in?

A) Including dance styles into her performances

B) Learning about different languages and cultures

C) Collecting musical instruments from around D) Hosting international food festivals

How does Taylor Swift express her love for vintage aesthetics?

A) By collecting antiques

B) By incorporating retro styles into her fashion, music videos, and album art

C) By exclusively using vintage musical instruments

D) By performing only historical songs

Answers

What aspect of global diversity has
Taylor Swift shown a keen interest in?

A) Including dance styles into her performances

**B) Learning about different languages and
cultures**

C) Collecting musical instruments from around D)
Hosting international food festivals

How does Taylor Swift express her love for vintage
aesthetics?

A) By collecting antiques

**B) By incorporating retro styles into her fashion,
music videos, and album art**

C) By exclusively using vintage musical
instruments

D) By performing only historical songs

DID YOU KNOW?

93. Taylor Swift's Acting Debut in "Valentine's Day"

Taylor Swift made her acting debut in the 2010 romantic comedy "Valentine's Day." Her appearance in this film showcased her talent beyond her established music career. "Valentine's Day" featured an ensemble cast, and Taylor Swift's role in the movie allowed her to explore another facet of her artistic abilities. This foray into acting was one of her early steps in branching out into different areas of entertainment, demonstrating her versatility and willingness to take on new challenges. Her participation in "Valentine's Day" was well-received and has been followed by other acting roles, further expanding her repertoire as a performer.

94. Taylor Swift's Historic Grammy Wins

Taylor Swift is the first female artist to win the Album of the Year Grammy Award three times. She made history with this achievement, which she earned for her albums "Fearless," "1989," and "Folklore." These wins highlight her exceptional talent as a musician and songwriter, as well as her influence and standing in the music industry. Each of these albums represents different phases in her career and showcases her ability to evolve and innovate musically. Taylor Swift's three Album of the Year Grammy wins are a testament to her enduring success and her ability to connect with audiences through her music.

DID YOU KNOW?

95. Burrito Beginnings: Taylor Swift's Late Adventure

In the 'Miss Americana' documentary, Taylor Swift revealed a surprising fact: she didn't try a burrito until she was 26 years old. This interesting tidbit gives us a peek into the life of the famous singer, who is known for writing songs that people can relate to and for being down-to-earth. The documentary takes us behind the scenes of her life and career, showing small, personal moments like this that prove Taylor is open to new experiences, even in her daily life. This story about her first time eating the popular Mexican food helps make Taylor seem more approachable and easy to relate to, bridging the gap between her and her fans.

96. Taylor Swift's Openness on Eating Disorders

In her documentary "Miss Americana," Taylor Swift openly shared her personal struggle with eating disorders, raising awareness and offering support to others who may also be dealing with similar health challenges. Her bravery in discussing such a sensitive topic highlights her dedication to advocacy and helping people feel less isolated in their struggles. Taylor's story serves as a powerful reminder of the significance of mental health and self-care.

DID YOU KNOW?

97. Music Video Setting for "Love Story"

The song "Love Story" by Taylor Swift features a music video with her wearing a gorgeous ball gown, dancing in a grand ballroom filled with mirrors. The video has a fairy tale-like setting and romantic visuals that perfectly match the song's narrative. The ballroom scene captures the essence of the song, creating a dreamy, romantic atmosphere that aligns with the theme of a love story that feels both timeless and magical. The mirrors in the ballroom add to the enchanting and elegant ambiance of the video, making it one of the most memorable and visually striking music videos in Taylor Swift's repertoire.

98. Taylor Swift's Grammy-Winning 2020 Album: "Folklore"

Taylor Swift's album, "Folklore," won the Grammy Award for Album of the Year in 2021. This album marked a significant stylistic shift for Taylor Swift, featuring more indie folk and alternative rock elements. "Folklore" received widespread acclaim for its introspective storytelling and atmospheric sound, showcasing Taylor's versatility as an artist and her ability to experiment with different musical styles. The album's success at the Grammy Awards, including winning Album of the Year, is a testament to its impact and resonance with both critics and audiences.

DID YOU KNOW?

99. Taylor Swift's Middle Name:

Taylor Swift was named after the singer-songwriter James Taylor, reflecting her parents' appreciation for music. Her full name is Taylor Alison Swift, with Alison being her middle name. It is often included when referencing her full legal name. Taylor Swift's name has become iconic in the music industry, synonymous with her successful career as a singer-songwriter.

100. Young Songwriting Talent Recognition:

At the age of 11, Taylor Swift won a national poetry contest with a poem titled "Monster in My Closet." This early achievement in writing showcased her creative talent and hinted at her future success as a songwriter. It reflects her innate ability to express thoughts and stories through words, a skill that would become central to her music career.

DID YOU KNOW?

101. Swift's Estates: Taylor's Multi-Million Dollar Real Estate Empire

Taylor Swift has made a name for herself in the real estate world, owning eight properties valued at over $81 million. Her impressive portfolio includes homes in Nashville, New York City, Rhode Island, and Los Angeles. These properties are not merely residences but also strategic investments, showcasing her business acumen. Taylor's choice of locations, from tranquil country settings to bustling city penthouses, demonstrates her flair for selecting prime real estate.

Hello There!

I hope you're having a great time with the Taylor Swift fact book. It's designed to be a delightful journey into the life and achievements of one of pop music's brightest stars. This book is brimming with fascinating facts and quizzes to deepen your knowledge of Taylor Swift's journey in music.

Your insights and experiences while reading this book matter a lot to us! If something new has caught your eye, or if a song of hers strikes a chord with you, we'd be thrilled to hear about it. Use the QR code to connect with others who have enjoyed this journey and share your own experiences and thoughts about the book.

Now, let's continue our to our bonus section of Taylor Swift's fascinating narrative together!

Let's see how much you've learned or already know, with some challenging quizzes to test your knowledge of Taylor Swift! Remember when we learned about those 350 hours of handwork that went into her tour outfits? Or how she broke the internet with millions vying for concert tickets? Lets test that big brain of yours.

Question 1: What is Taylor Swift's middle name?
A) Elizabeth
B) Alison
C) Marie
D) Anne

Question 2: Taylor Swift's 2020 album, "_____," won the Grammy Award for Album of the Year in 2021.

Question 3: Which movie did Taylor Swift make her acting debut in?
A) "Valentine's Day"
B) "The Giver"
C) "Cats"
D) "The Lorax"

Question 4: Which song did Taylor Swift collaborate on with Ed Sheeran and Future?
A) "Everything Has Changed"
B) "End Game"
C) "Me!"
D) "I Don't Wanna Live Forever"

Question 5: Which Taylor Swift song was featured in "The Hunger Games" movie soundtrack?
A) "Safe & Sound"
B) "Eyes Open"
C) "Today Was a Fairytale"
D) "Sweeter Than Fiction"

Question 6: When did Taylor Swift become the youngest-ever winner of the Grammy for Album of the Year?
A) 18
B) 20
C) 22
D) 24

Question 7: Which city is Taylor Swift originally from?
A) Nashville, Tennessee
B) Reading, Pennsylvania
C) New York City, New York
D) Los Angeles, California

Question 8: Who did Taylor Swift name as her biggest musical influence?
A) Bruce Springsteen
B) Paul McCartney
C) Shania Twain
D) Madonna

Question 9: Which famous supermodel appeared in Taylor Swift's music video for "Bad Blood"?
A) Gigi Hadid
B) Cara Delevingne
C) Naomi Campbell
D) Kate Moss

Question 10: Which album did Taylor Swift release in 2014, featuring the hit single "Shake It Off"?
A) "Lover"
B) "Reputation"
C) "1989"
D) "Folklore"

Question 11: What inspired Taylor Swift and Brendon Urie's 'ME!' song?
A) A dream
B) A breakup
C) A fantasy world
D) Taylor's personality

Question 12: Which Taylor Swift album made her the first female artist to have six albums each sell over a million copies in its first week?
A) "Reputation"
B) "1989"
C) "Lover"
D) "Folklore"

Question 13: At what age did Taylor Swift sign her first record deal?
A) 14
B) 15
C) 16
D) 17

Question 14: How
many cars does Taylor Swift own?
A) 1-2
B) 3-4
C) 5-6
D) More than 7

Question 15: What was the name of Taylor
Swift's first world tour?
A) The Fearless Tour
B) The Red Tour
C) The Speak Now World Tour
D) The 1989 World Tour

Question 16: Taylor Swift has been vocal about
which political issue?
A) Climate change
B) LGBTQ+ rights
C) Education reform
D) All of the above

Question 17:Taylor Swift collaborated with which
legendary folk artist on her album "Evermore"?
A) Bob Dylan
B) Joni Mitchell
C) Bon Iver
D) James Taylor

Question 18: What hobby

did Taylor Swift particularly enjoy during her childhood, which is often reflected in her songwriting?
A) Painting
B) Horseback riding
C) Creative writing
D) Acting

Question 19: Which song did Taylor Swift perform during the 2010 Grammy Awards that marked a significant moment in her early career?
A) "Fearless"
B) "You Belong With Me"
C) "Fifteen"
D) "White Horse"

Question 20: Taylor Swift once said, "No matter what happens in life, be good to people. Being good to people is a wonderful legacy to leave behind." In which context did she say this?
A) In a magazine interview
B) During a concert
C) In her documentary "Miss Americana"
D) Accepting an award

Answers

QUESTION 1.
B)
Explanation: Taylor Swift's full name is Taylor Alison Swift. She was named after the singer-songwriter James Taylor.

QUESTION 2.
"Folklore"
Explanation: This album marked a significant stylistic shift for Taylor, featuring more indie folk and alternative rock elements.

QUESTION 3.
A)
Explanation: Taylor Swift made her acting debut in the 2010 romantic comedy "Valentine's Day," showcasing her talent beyond music.

QUESTION 4.
B)
Explanation: "End Game," a track from Taylor Swift's "Reputation" album, features collaborations with Ed Sheeran and Future, blending different musical styles.

QUESTION 5.
A)

*Explanation: "Safe & Sound,"
featuring The Civil Wars, was part of
"The Hunger Games" soundtrack, showcasing
Taylor Swift's versatility as an artist.*

QUESTION 6.
B)

*Explanation: Taylor Swift won the Grammy for
Album of the Year for "Fearless" at age 20,
becoming the youngest artist at the time to
win this prestigious award.*

QUESTION 7.
B)

*Explanation: Taylor Swift was born and raised
in Reading, Pennsylvania, before moving to
Nashville, Tennessee, to pursue her music
career.*

QUESTION 8.
C)

*Explanation: Taylor Swift has frequently named
Shania Twain as her biggest musical influence,
citing Twain's ability to blend country and pop
music as a significant inspiration for her own
career.*

QUESTION 9.

A)

Explanation: "Lover," released in 2019, is Taylor Swift's seventh studio album, featuring a colorful and romantic aesthetic distinct from her previous work.

Question 10:
C) A fantasy world

Explanation: Taylor Swift and Brendon Urie's song 'ME!' is inspired by the concept of a fantasy world. It celebrates individuality and self-confidence, with its upbeat tone and colorful imagery reflecting a whimsical, fantasy-like theme.

Question 12:
B) "1989"

Explanation: Taylor Swift's album "1989" made her the first female artist to have six albums each sell over a million copies in their first week. This milestone solidified her status as a pop music icon.

Question 13:
B) 15

Explanation: Taylor Swift signed her first record deal at the age of 15, marking the start of her meteoric rise in the music industry and setting the foundation for her successful career.

Question 14:
B) 3-4

Explanation: Taylor Swift owns between 3 and 4 cars, showcasing her love for vehicles and adding to the many facets of her glamorous lifestyle.

Question 15:
A) The Fearless Tour

Explanation: Taylor Swift's first world tour was "The Fearless Tour," which promoted her album "Fearless" and helped establish her as a global superstar in the music scene.

Question 16:
D) All of the above

Explanation: Taylor Swift has been vocal about several political issues, including climate change, LGBTQ+ rights, and education reform, demonstrating her commitment to using her platform to advocate for various causes.

Question 17:
C) Bon Iver

Explanation: On her album "Evermore," Taylor Swift collaborated with the legendary folk band Bon Iver, especially on the song "Exile," showcasing her versatility

and depth as an
artist.

Question 18:
C) Creative writing

Explanation: Taylor Swift enjoyed creative
writing during her childhood, which is often
reflected in her songwriting. Her ability to tell
stories through her lyrics is a testament to her
early love for writing.

Question 19:
C) "Fifteen"

Explanation: Taylor Swift performed "Fifteen"
at the 2010 Grammy Awards, a significant
moment in her early career that highlighted
her storytelling ability and connected with fans
worldwide.

Question 20:
A) In a magazine interview

Explanation: Taylor Swift's quote about
being good to people was made in a magazine
interview, reflecting her philosophy of kindness
and the importance of leaving a positive legacy.

Well you've made it to the end, and get to see me writing this book up :).

We've been on an incredible ourney together, filled with wonder and excitement, just like waiting for the next big Taylor Swift album to drop. It's been a thrilling ride, and I'm curious to find out what parts of our adventure stood out to you the most.

Did any of the trivia catch you by surprise, or perhaps you discovered a new favorite story about Taylor? Your thoughts and discoveries are like the beautiful music to the words in our book, making the story richer and more vibrant. I'd love to hear what you thought about our journey and what you're hoping to see next. Feel free to share your insights by using the QR code – it's like leaving a note in our secret Swiftie diary!

Thank you so much for joining in this celebration of all things Taylor Swift. Your imagination and curiosity turn these pages into a living, breathing tale of musical genius and pop culture magic. Even though we're turning the final page of this book, Taylor's incredible journey is far from over, and your excitement is the spark that ignites our creativity for future projects.

As we wrap up this chapter, let's keep our curiosity burning bright. Who knows where our exploration of Taylor Swift's ever-changing world will take us next? Until we meet again in the pages of her unfolding story, keep your Swiftie playlist on repeat and the fun facts coming. Let's continue to celebrate the music and the moments that make Taylor Swift an unforgettable icon!

Printed in Great Britain
by Amazon

41913699R00046